Gloucester

Gloucester

RECREATING THE PAST

Philip Moss & Andrew Armstrong

FOR THE GLOUCESTER HISTORY FESTIVAL

First published 2021
Reprinted 2024

The History Press
97 St George's Place, Cheltenham,
Gloucestershire, GL50 3QB
www.thehistorypress.co.uk

British Library Cataloguing in Publication Data.
A catalogue record for this book is available from the British Library.

ISBN 978 0 7509 9790 4

Typesetting and origination by The History Press
Printed by TJ Books Limited, Padstow, Cornwall

Contents

About the Authors

PHILIP MOSS was born in Gloucester and educated at the Crypt Grammar School. He studied technical illustration at the Gloucester College of Art and the Royal West of England Academy of Art at Bristol. He worked in technical publications in the aviation and construction equipment industries, and later as a freelance illustrator and designer. He was involved in many projects in engineering, architecture and also archaeology with the recording and publication of many sites, not only locally but also of Carthage and Rome.

   He was a founding member of the Gloucester and District Archaeological Research Group in 1967 and of the Gloucester Civic Trust in 1972. He was awarded the Mayor of Gloucester's Medal in 2016 for his work in promoting the heritage of the city.

ANDREW ARMSTRONG was born in Colchester and spent his childhood moving between various army bases in Germany and England before settling in Salisbury. He graduated with a degree in archaeology from the University of York in 2000. Uncertain what to do with his life, but horrified by the concept of an office job, he tried his hand at being a 'field archaeologist', spending six years working on archaeological sites throughout southern England. This was followed by a brief but educational period as an archaeological consultant, and something called a 'countryside archaeological adviser' at Gloucestershire County Council. He joined Gloucester City Council as City Archaeologist in 2012. After nine years Andrew is starting to feel like he knows what he's doing, which may not be a good sign.

Acknowledgements

Over the years I have had, and still have, the pleasure of working with many archaeologists and historians, notably Henry Hurst, Carolyn Heighway, John Rhodes, Malcolm Atkin, Nigel Spry, Hugh Conway-Jones, Tony Conder and Malcolm Watkins.

Thanks to my wife, Gillian, for all her help and encouragement on many archaeological projects.

All the illustrations were drawn using the known archaeological and historical information available at the time. However, as new evidence comes to light, I hope others will be moved to reinterpret the drawings featured in this book.

It has been an enjoyable and rewarding experience to work with Andrew Armstrong in the compilation of this work. His knowledge and enthusiasm are a major asset to the City of Gloucester.

Philip Moss

Many of the photographs or images reproduced in this book were kindly provided by the Museum of Gloucester. The authors are also grateful to the following for permission to reproduce images: Gloucestershire Archives, Gloucestershire County Council Archaeology Service, Avon Archaeology, Cotswold Archaeology, Henry Hurst, Cape Homes, Ted Wilson, Llanthony Secunda Priory Trust and Reach PLC. Finally, I'm very grateful to my wife Tamsen for proof-reading the drafts of this book; she has heroically filtered out my jargon-heavy text and patiently identified a number of regrettable typos – thank heavens for English Literature graduates!

Andrew Armstrong

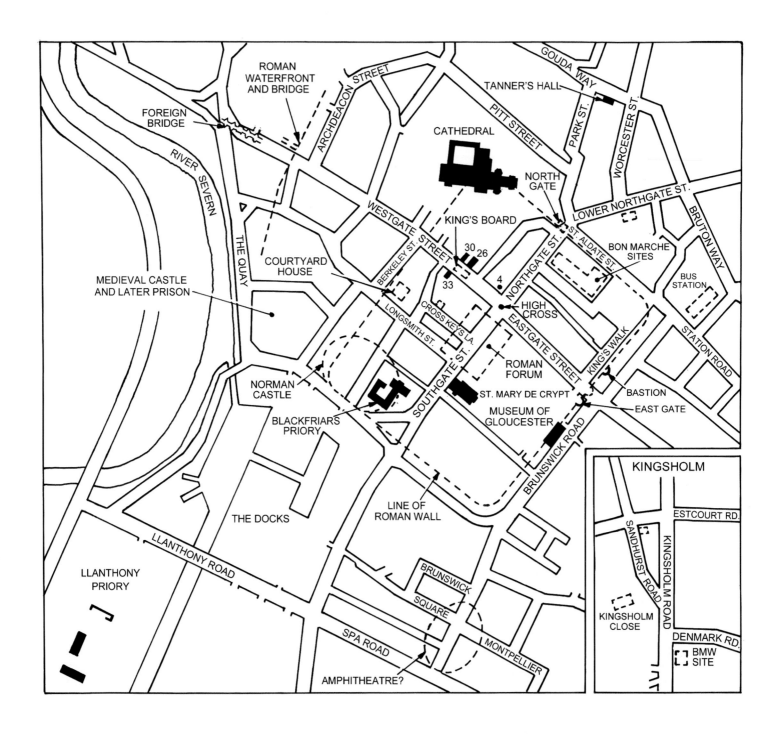

Introduction

If you stand today at the Cross in the centre of Gloucester, you are on a man-made hill, perhaps 4 to 5m above the original ground level. Below you lie layer after layer of the city's history. If you'd stood on the same spot nearly two thousand years ago you may well have seen the arrival of the first Roman soldiers on the edge of the Severn, or the creation of the fortress that was to become Gloucester.

The military engineers who laid out that fortress were, unknowingly, defining the layout of a city that still endures after two thousand years. Many of the roads and streets in the city today were defined by the Romans and still broadly follow their original routes. The fortress remained in use for some decades and was replaced ultimately by a newly founded Roman city. That city, called Glevum, was a 'colonia' – a retirement settlement for Roman soldiers. By this time (the late first century AD), the term 'Roman' could refer to people from a diverse range of countries and backgrounds and it is likely that this first Gloucester was populated by people from all over the Mediterranean world, as well as parts of Germany and northern France.

These early citizens adopted for their city the exact layout of the fortress from which it had grown. For around three hundred years, they raised public buildings, built town houses, prayed to various gods, died and were buried. But then their city, like the empire that had borne it, began to decline. By the sixth century it is unclear if Glevum still survived as a city. If not, it may still have been a place of importance, a site perhaps of political and religious leadership. A small population living on in the faded grandeur of Rome.

With the coming of the seventh century, Gloucester emerges from the Dark Ages back into recorded history. Minor princes, lords of the forgotten Kingdom of the Hwicce, saw fit to found a minster (the Anglo-Saxon name for a monastery) in

Gloucester. These Hiwccan lords were vassals of a greater power – the Kingdom of Mercia. For a time, Mercia was the greatest English kingdom, whose hegemony extended from Kent into Wales and as far north as the Humber.

In AD 865 the Danes (Vikings, if you prefer) invaded and conquered half of England, including the north-eastern half of Mercia. Gloucester, in the south-west of Mercia, remained English. The Danish great army, led by a king called Guthrum, occupied Gloucester for some months. Somehow, Gloucester endured these disasters and emerged from the conflict with newfound importance.

Alfred the Great, King of Wessex*, was able to defeat Guthrum's army and to stop any further Danish conquest. Consequently, at the end of the ninth century Gloucester found itself the capital city of English Mercia, ruled by a daughter of Alfred the Great – Aethelflaed. It is from Gloucester that Aethelflaed reconquered the kingdom of Mercia from the Danes. Gloucester was also childhood home to Athelstan – a monarch somewhat lost to history, who was to be the first king of all the English peoples. He died in Gloucester in AD 939. Gloucester remained a royal city in the later Saxon period and was a favoured haunt of Edward the Confessor.

After the Norman conquest of 1066, Gloucester continued to attract kings and was the place from which William the Conqueror commissioned Domesday Book, that extraordinary glimpse of the England of a thousand years ago. Although not obvious today, two castles were built in the city. The first, a timber and earth structure that lies partly beneath Blackfriars, was replaced by a more impressive stone keep and bailey on the site of what was later Gloucester prison. The Normans built prodigiously in the years after the invasion, raising the churches and monasteries that can be found throughout the city today.

Henry III was crowned in St Peter's Abbey in Gloucester in 1216 during the turmoil of the first Barons' War – a conflict between his father, King John, and the great lords of England. He remained fond of the city, repairing and reinforcing its walls, greatly

*A southern English kingdom – by the late ninth century it controlled all the land south of the Thames.

improving the castle and endowing the various religious houses over the next sixty years. He was often in residence, as was his son, the future Edward I.

After Edward, few royals took much interest in Gloucester. Richard III granted the city's charter of incorporation in 1483, essentially giving the citizens the right to manage their own affairs. This was in gratitude after Gloucester had closed its gates to Margaret of Anjou, the leader of Lancastrian forces seeking to reach allies in Wales. Instead, the trapped Lancastrian army faced annihilation at the battle of Tewkesbury – one of the bloodiest battles of the War of the Roses.

The attention of monarchs returned to Gloucester during the English Civil War. In 1643, after the Royalist army had defeated all other Parliamentary forces in south-west England, Charles I himself came to Gloucester. He hoped to quickly subdue the city, gather his forces and march on London and perhaps win the war. The failure of his army and his ambitions in the muddy, flooded fields around Gloucester in August and September was a major turning point of the war – from which the Royalist cause never recovered.

The story of Gloucester, a fortress city on the Severn, has, in so many ways, been the story of England. It is an extraordinary story – one that archaeologists and historians struggle to convey and to articulate in a way that does justice to achievements, events or monuments. Thank heavens then, that we have the artwork of Phil Moss to help us. Over the last forty years Phil has produced work that inspires a better and more empathetic understanding of that story. Phil's wonderful artistic skill, combined with his real archaeological and historical knowledge, mean that he has been able to convey Gloucester's past in a way that few people could, recreating this past in way that lets us better comprehend our history and, hopefully, better appreciate our present.

Beginnings

Gloucester was founded by the Romans, who landed in Kent in AD 43 and had reached the edge of the Severn by about AD 47. On their arrival, the Roman army built their first fortress – not in the city centre, but in Kingsholm, a suburb about a kilometre to the north. What attracted the Romans to Kingsholm? Well, I hear you cry – it's a perfectly pleasant spot, nice rugby ground, good schools that sort of thing. Of course, in Roman times Kingsholm was, as far as we can tell, a slightly raised meadow next to the river and was no doubt damp and prone to flooding. It is a puzzling location for the first fortress in Gloucester, low-lying and some distance from the best river crossing.

Excavations at Kingsholm Close in 1972.

So why *did* the Romans build their first fort in Kingsholm? Well, recent archaeological excavations further south in the city centre have found the remains of a late Iron Age settlement, which may have been standing when the Romans arrived. The people who lived there would have been part of a nation the Romans referred to as the 'Dubonni', who were allies of Rome. It is possible, therefore, that the first Roman fortress was located at Kingsholm to avoid antagonising these friendly locals.

Above: Sandhurst Road – excavation of the Roman fortress bank in 1985.
Left: The fortress defensive ditch as excavated (and full of water).

Archaeologists first found evidence for this earlier fortress in 1972, when excavations in Kingsholm Close found the remains of military equipment and buildings.

While this was clear evidence of military activity, it did not give archaeologists much idea of the extent or layout of the fortress. This remained something of a mystery until 1985, when archaeologists excavating in Sandhurst Road found part of the fortress defences, formed of an earthen bank and a large defensive ditch. This defined the northern edge of the fortress, and from this it was possible to estimate the extent of the fort.

Our understanding was further improved in 1987 when excavations on Kingsholm Road (on what was to become the Richard Cound car showroom) found the remains of a civilian settlement located to the south of the fort. Unofficial settlements like this are often found near Roman forts (archaeologists sometimes refer to such a settlement as a 'vicus'). This reconstruction drawing was commissioned by the Richard Cound BMW car dealership for a commemorative brochure on the opening of their new showroom 1987. The view faces north towards what would have been the southern gate of the fort.

Kingsholm Fortress at some point after AD 47.

The New Fortress

The new Roman fortress in Gloucester in the mid to late first century.

Perhaps ten years later, around AD 57, the Roman army decided to build a new fortress further south, in what was to become Gloucester. So, why move the fort to this location? Well, the key reason was probably control of the River Severn. Moving the location of the fort to what is now Gloucester city centre allowed the Roman army to control both the river crossing and movement up and down the river.

The new fortress at Gloucester was laid out following some well-established Roman military principles: The fortress headquarters (known as the 'principia') was always at the centre of the fort. In modern-day Gloucester it is situated at the top of Southgate Street, just below the Cross. This was a carefully selected site; if you stand on the Cross today, you can see that you are actually on a hill. This is especially visible as you look down Westgate Street. The principia was situated so that much of the camp, and especially the gates, would be visible from it.

This new fortress was larger than the earlier one at Kingsholm and probably remained in use for twenty to thirty years. The reconstruction drawing on page 17 shows a small civilian settlement extending northwards along modern-day Kingsholm Road and London Road. The old fortress at Kingsholm is visible in the background.

An excavation on Berkeley Street in 1969 has given us our best glimpse of this second fortress. Archaeologists found the remains of long barrack blocks similar to those found in other fortresses of this time. These barrack buildings were well made – evidence was found for wall plaster for example – but temporary, having only a timber frame and foundations. They were later replaced with more substantial, long-term structures.

The photograph shows the remains of one of the early barrack buildings found during that excavation. The timbers that would have formed the foundation have rotted away and what remains is the foundation cut of the original building, which indicates its layout.

The excavated footings of a Roman barrack building found in Berkeley Street in 1969.

The fortress was enclosed by a defensive rampart, the remains of which have been found by archaeologists in a number of locations around the city.

This reconstruction drawing shows how the rampart was constructed. The bank of the rampart was formed out of a mix of the local clay and gravel. Turves were laid along the faces of the bank to prevent erosion.

Because the ground was so wet, the Romans founded the defensive bank on split timber slats laid in horizontal layers. Despite being two thousand years old, the timbers have survived in waterlogged conditions where there is no oxygen. The photograph on the following page shows these timbers as found during an excavation in 1969.

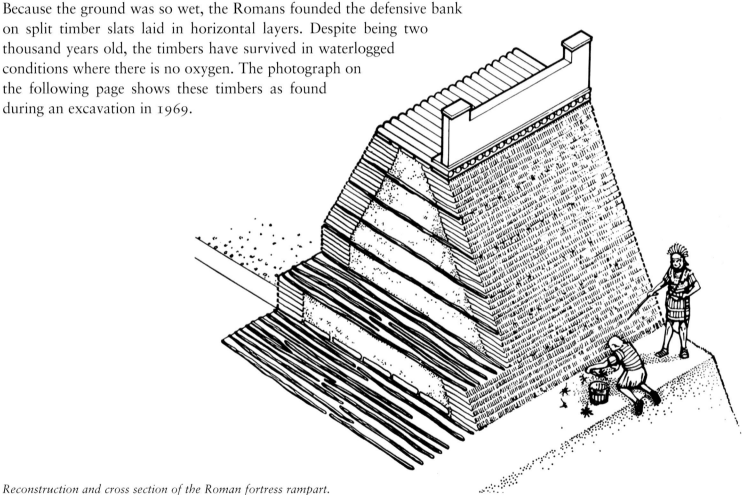

Reconstruction and cross section of the Roman fortress rampart.

Two thousand-year-old timber slats, found beneath the King's Walk shopping centre in 1969.

At the end of each of the four main roads of the fortress was a gate. The eastern and northern gatehouses have been excavated by archaeologists. Both gatehouses were made of timber and, due to the wet conditions on site, some of the fortress timbers actually survived. The reconstruction drawing (opposite) shows the Roman east gate as it would have looked in the late first century` based on the archaeological evidence and comparison with other Roman forts.

The east gate of the Roman fortress in the late first century AD.

Colonia

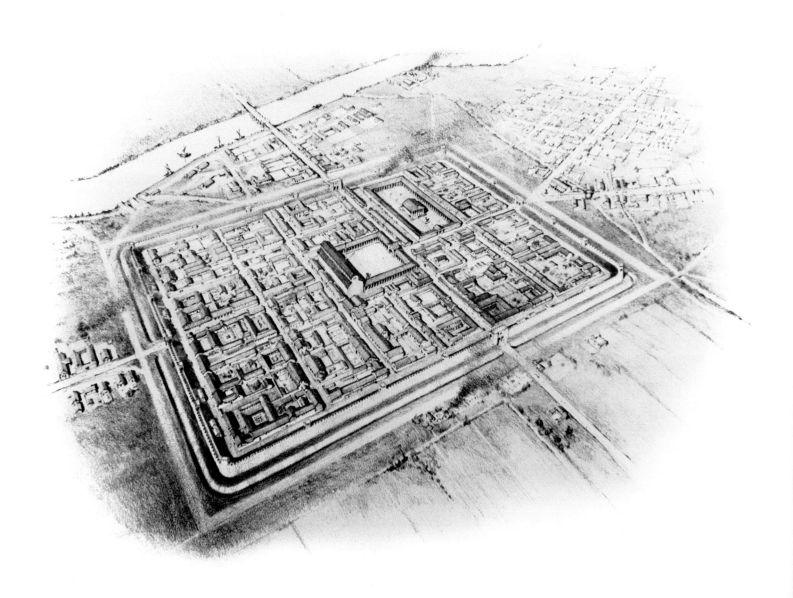

In the late first century AD, the fortress in Gloucester went out of use and a new city was founded on the same spot. This was a special type of city, a colonia, founded as a settlement for retired soldiers. We are not certain exactly when it was founded – definitely between AD 80 and 110, and probably between AD 96 and 98. This date is given in part from archaeological evidence, but also from historical sources: in this case, a tombstone found in Rome in which the Roman name of the city 'Colonia Glevum' is given the title 'Ner', thought to relate to the Emperor Nerva. This would suggest that the city was founded during Nerva's reign, which was very short. He was only in office between AD 96 and 98.

At the time there were only two other 'colonia' in Britain – at Colchester and Lincoln. The Roman authorities tended to locate colonia in important strategic locations where large numbers of loyal, militarily trained locals were a helpful insurance. The site of Gloucester was probably chosen because it was a key river crossing and supply route.

The new city was founded exactly on the footprint of the old fortress, using the same roads and the same boundary. The archaeological evidence shows that the first citizens of Gloucester, or 'Glevum' as it was known, actually lived, at first, in the old military barrack blocks, which they gradually converted into civilian homes.

Opposite: The Roman colonia of Glevum in the second century AD.

Right: Archaeological excavations in Berkeley Street in 1969.

Reconstruction of the Roman courtyard house found at Berkeley Street.

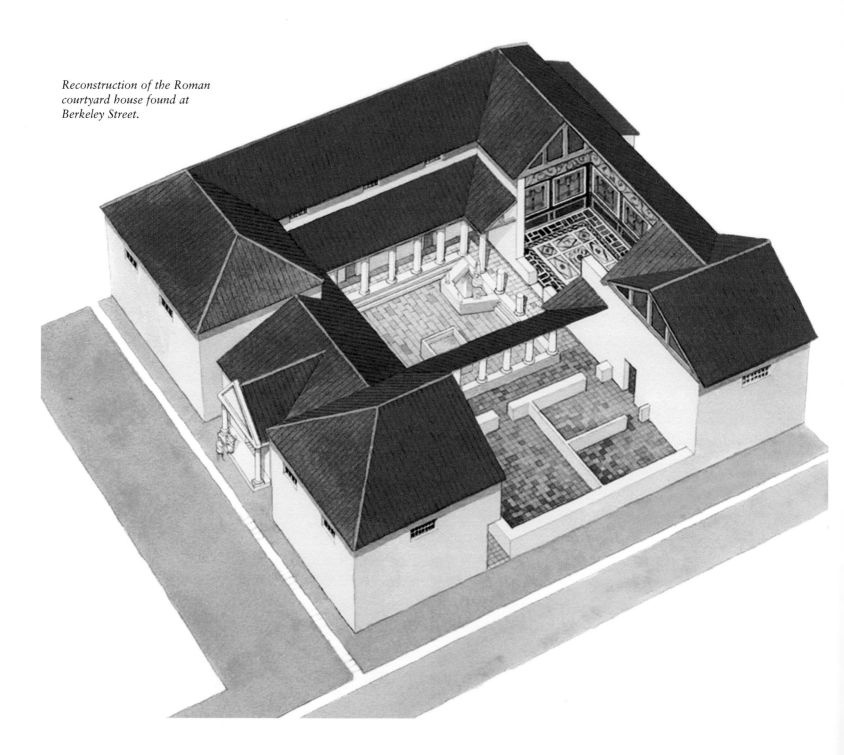

The reconstruction drawing on page 22 shows the city as it may have looked in the middle of the second century. By this time the walled area of the city was well developed with town houses and public buildings. Suburbs are developing to the north, west and south.

So, what kind of city did those new citizens make?

Over the next three hundred years, the citizens of Glevum built themselves increasingly impressive town houses. One of the best examples was found in 1969 on the site of what is now the telephone exchange on Berkeley Street.

This would have been an impressive and high-status residence with a central courtyard. It would have been very Mediterranean in style, although, in deference to the climate, far smaller than would be found in the south of France or Italy. Archaeologists found the remains of a fountain in the courtyard with a large water cistern just next to it. The remains of a mosaic floor surface were found in one room and large amounts of decorated wall plaster were found throughout the site. It is assumed from the size of the foundations that there was also an upper floor to this building.

The reconstruction drawing opposite shows how it may have looked; one of several courtyarded town houses we find in the south-western corner of the city. It would, internally at least, have been a very colourful building.

These very important remains were excavated at a time before archaeology was protected as part of the planning system. So, while the archaeologists and volunteers did a brilliant job, sadly at the end of their work, those remains they had not been able to excavate were destroyed. Today, it would be very rare to destroy such important archaeological remains and never without excavation.

Holes into the Past

Some of our best evidence about life in the Roman colonia of Glevum has come from the site of the former Debenhams department store, which sits between the Oxbode and St Aldates Street fronting onto King's Square. This used to be a Bon Marché department store and it was developed and expanded over the course of the twentieth century, with each new extension apparently requiring a basement. Each new basement exposed, and sadly quite often destroyed, evidence of interesting and impressive buildings within the Roman city.

In 1914 an exceptionally beautiful mosaic pavement was found and presented to the Museum of Gloucester. It still survives today, set into the floor of the museum.

This is the only surviving complete (or very nearly complete) mosaic in the city. It gives a hint of how impressive and colourful some of these town houses must have been.

The Bon Marché Mosaic, found in 1914.

In the 1930s, further building works were undertaken and members of the Gloucester Roman Research Committee (a forerunner of later archaeological societies in the city) were able to watch construction works with permission from the builders. This is not an ideal way to work for an archaeologist, as the archaeological remains were often destroyed as they were found. That said, some impressive evidence for the Roman colonia was uncovered. The archaeologists found further mosaics, the remains of hypocausts (a kind of underfloor heating system), stone columns and wells for water.

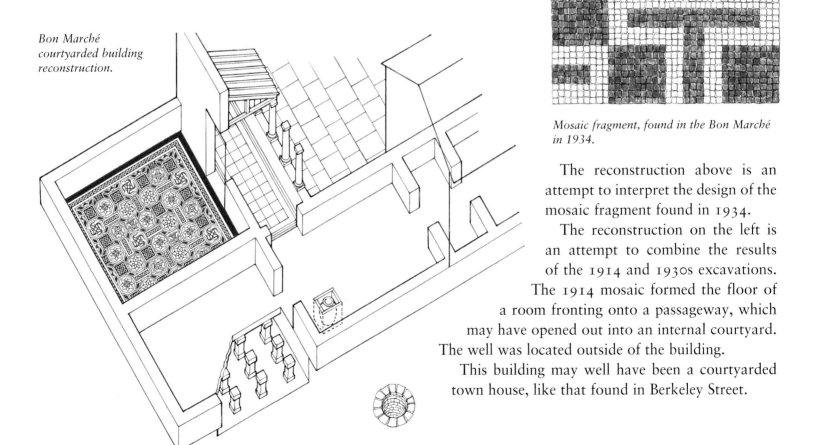

Bon Marché courtyarded building reconstruction.

Mosaic fragment, found in the Bon Marché in 1934.

The reconstruction above is an attempt to interpret the design of the mosaic fragment found in 1934.

The reconstruction on the left is an attempt to combine the results of the 1914 and 1930s excavations. The 1914 mosaic formed the floor of a room fronting onto a passageway, which may have opened out into an internal courtyard. The well was located outside of the building.

This building may well have been a courtyarded town house, like that found in Berkeley Street.

Return to the Bon Marché

In 1955, staff from the city museum were called out to yet more construction work on the same site. Works were being undertaken to extend the cellars beneath the store. By the time they arrived on site, a very great deal of damage had already been done. The archaeologists found the fragmentary remains of walls and floor surfaces and a rather beautiful well head. Two damaged mosaic pavements were also noted, no doubt similar to the one found in 1914. Sadly, as the photograph below shows, these were damaged before the archaeologists got to the site and were subsequently lost. This demonstrates very clearly why archaeology needs to be protected in the planning system. Back in 1955, and more recently, a developer could simply dig a hole through hugely important archaeological remains and destroy them at will, provided they owned the property.

Bon Marché excavations 1955 showing a damaged mosaic.

Archaeologists could only get onto site with permission and only excavate by agreement. As you can imagine, over the course of the 1950s, '60s and '70s, this lack of protection caused the destruction of a huge amount of archaeology throughout Britain. Even where archaeologists were able to excavate, their work was often hurried and partial. In many cases, such sites have never been written up or published because the funding has never been available. Therefore, the information they uncovered has never been recorded or shared, which is a great loss to our understanding of history.

In 1958, the managers of the Bon Marché once again chose to extend their store. Thankfully, the Museum of Gloucester Archaeological Assistant, A.G. Hunter, was on hand to undertake a volunteer excavation.

The building found here was, judging by its layout, a shop or possibly an eating establishment. It was right next

door to the townhouse found in the 1930s. The building was street-facing on two sides, with a covered veranda extending out onto the street. Archaeologists found the remains of a hearth and at least two ovens. A room to the rear had yet another mosaic.

Thought to be the only known photograph the of Bon Marché 'star and flower' mosaic found in 1961.

Reconstruction drawing of a possible Roman eating establishment, found on the Bon Marché site in 1958.

The reconstruction drawing opposite shows the building as a single-storey eating establishment open to the street at one end. A similar building, again with an oven, has been found beneath Westgate Street. Roman Gloucester, as now, must have had a wide selection of eating establishments, pubs and inns.

Between 1958 and 1961, archaeologists kept watch on the works in the Bon Marché but despite their best efforts, important and beautiful remains were lost. Perhaps most sadly was a mosaic last seen in 1961 with the design of a star around a flower (see p29). There is no confirmed evidence about what happened to the mosaic (which really was stunning) but it was almost certainly destroyed. Over the whole period from 1914, works on the Bon Marché site exposed at least four remarkable mosaics, of which only one was saved. With a bit more protection all four of those mosaics could now be in the Museum of Gloucester forming an extraordinary centre point for the Roman exhibitions. The fact that only one survives is a dreadful loss both to art history and the city.

Another fragment of mosaic found in 1961.

The Forum

While the citizens of Glevum built new homes, the civic administration undertook some large public building projects. Of these, one of the earliest and most impressive was a space known as the forum in the centre of the city, at the top end of what is now Southgate Street.

The forum was a large, open space, surrounded on three sides by a colonnaded enclosure with an entrance to the north. The southern edge was formed by a large public building called the Forum Basilica, a kind of combined council office, town hall and temple.

The remains of Gloucester's forum were found during an excavation in 1968–69. The archaeologists, as ever, were seeking to record what they could before building works destroyed more of the city's past. In this case, the development was the new Eastgate shopping centre. This particular excavation was, confusingly, by the Southgate entrance. Although the remains were badly damaged, the archaeologists found evidence for an imposing public space, which must have looked very impressive.

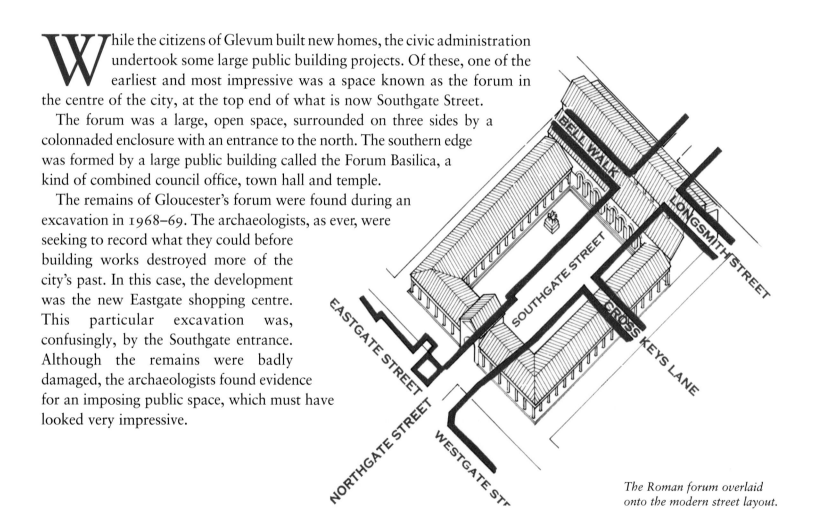

The Roman forum overlaid onto the modern street layout.

The forum was large; larger than many examples in Italy, measuring about 100m by 67m and running from just below the Cross as far south as the modern-day shopping centre entrance. The drawing on the following page is an isometric view of the south-east corner. The archaeological evidence suggests that the forum was constructed soon after the establishment of the colonia.

The open space of the forum was paved with large Forest of Dean sandstone slabs, while the architectural stone was Cotswold limestone.

Fascinatingly, the archaeologists found the remains of a bronze statue of a figure on horseback, which was probably located on a large stone plinth in the south-east corner of the forum. This statue, which was scaled at twice life size, may have been one of a pair flanking the entrance to the basilica. It may well have been the representation of an emperor, possibly Nerva.

Above: Excavation of the Roman forum in 1968–69. (Permission H. Hurst)
Right: Paving slabs found during excavation in 1968–69. (Permission H. Hurst)

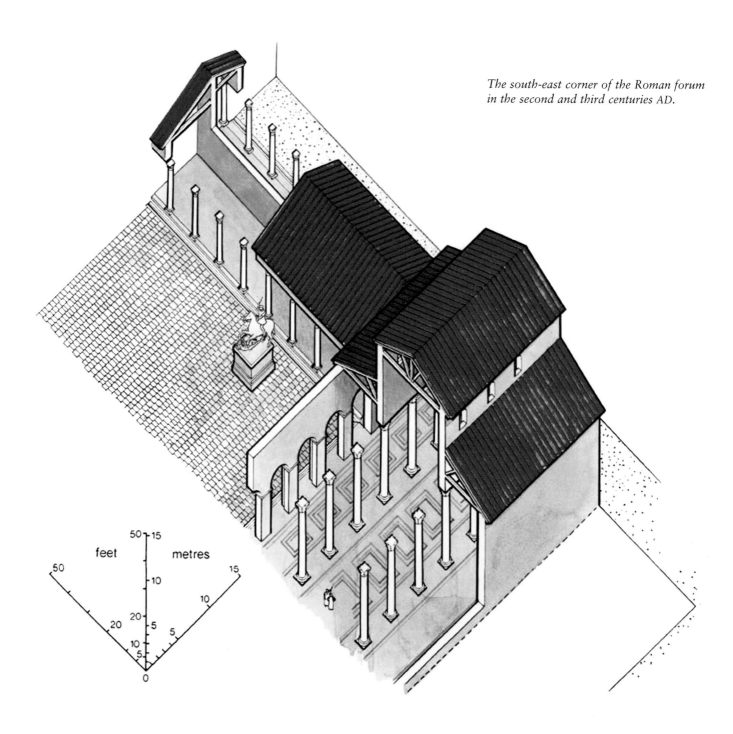

The south-east corner of the Roman forum in the second and third centuries AD.

feet   metres

Above left: Reconstruction of how the equine statue may have looked.
Below left: Alternative interpretation of how the statue may have looked.
Above right: The modern day Nerva statue on Southgate Street.

Today, if you wander down Southgate Street, you will see a reconstruction of this statue close to the spot where the original was found. Nerva is one of the lesser-known Roman emperors but he did a good job in difficult conditions; taking over from the unpopular Domitian and avoiding civil war – so it is nice to see him remembered in the city that may have borne his name.

The Forum Basilica façade seen from the north.

This is a reconstruction of how the forum basilica may have looked, probably in the second century AD. It has been suggested that the basilica would be about the same size as the cathedral nave. The basilica is thought to have been fronted with an arcade, a row of arches that would have made the building accessible from the forum.

The basilica was the very heart of the civic administration in the city, the place where public business would have been discussed and decided.

Stonework in Southgate Street

In 2018, archaeologists uncovered a reminder of just how important this part of Roman Glevum was. Two large fragments of Roman stone were revealed during work in front of St Mary De Crypt Church in Southgate Street, just south of the forum basilica. One piece of stone was part of a cornice, a projecting ornament carved with leaves and scrollwork. The fragment is very large, nearly a metre long, and it must have come from a very substantial building.

The second piece of stone is less decorated, but still important as it is actually the upper portion of a Roman altar. Sadly, we are missing the front of the altar, so there is no inscription. The back of the altar is quite rough, so it was probably mounted onto the front of a wall or building and designed to be seen from one side.

These two fragments may have come from the forum basilica itself, or perhaps from a nearby temple. Either way, they give some idea of the grandeur of public buildings in Glevum and hint at what still remains to be discovered beneath the streets of the city.

Left: Carved cornice fragment found beneath Southgate Street in 2018. (Avon Archaeology)

Right: Altar fragment found beneath Southgate Street in 2018. (Avon Archaeology)

Westgate Colonnade

Another example of impressive public buildings in Glevum has been found along the north side of what is today Westgate Street. Archaeologists have uncovered a series of enormous stone columns running in a line along the northern edge of modern-day Westgate Street. Perhaps five of these have been found to date and more are hinted at in historic texts. They extend for over 100m, running from the junction of the main Roman roads to the western city walls. The best example was found at 4 Westgate Street in 1971 and you can still see the foundation stone today in the window of HSBC.

After the column was found, it was moved and can now be seen in the Museum of Gloucester just next to the reception desk. It is over 80cm in diameter and was still standing to nearly 2m in height when found.

Left: Excavation of the stone column at 4 Westgate Street in 1971.

Opposite: The column today in the reception of the Museum of Gloucester. (Museum of Gloucester)

This column is carved from limestone originating in the Painswick area. These had to be quarried, carved and transported to Gloucester, and there were probably at least twelve columns. This must have been a huge undertaking and gives us some idea of the sheer scale of Roman Glevum.

Frustratingly, we do not really know what these columns were. One theory is that we are looking at a massive colonnade, either freestanding (as are seen in some Roman cities in the Mediterranean) or forming part of a larger building or complex of buildings. Some archaeologists have argued that there was a public bath complex to the north of Westgate Street or perhaps a temple complex.

The Walls

After founding the city, the citizens and magistrates of Glevum gradually replaced the earth and timber banks of the old fortress with proper stone walls over the course of three hundred years. They initially seem to have faced the earthen fortress bank with stone but gradually, during the third and fourth centuries especially, a more substantial wall was created. The third century was a time of exceptional upheaval and civil war in the Roman Empire, so strong walls may have suddenly become important.

Reconstructions showing various phases of the city walls – the evidence suggests that the walls were improved incrementally over hundreds of years.

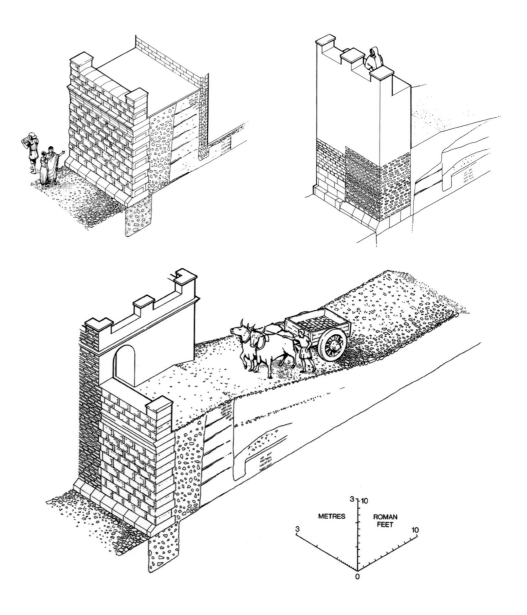

METRES | ROMAN FEET

A length of the Roman wall exposed during excavations at the east gate in 1974 (By permission Ted Wilson)

Wooden stakes, driven into the natural clays to act as a foundation for the Roman wall (from excavations in the east gate in 1974). (Permission Ted Wilson)

As well as this practical reason for improvement, the wall may have had a legal and religious function and, of course, it was a symbol of civic pride.

The problem with trying to build walls (or indeed anything) in Roman Glevum was sourcing building stone. Gloucester is located on a low hill of soggy gravel overlying clay. The nearest quality building stone is limestone from Robinswood Hill or Painswick, some kilometres east of the city. In the second century, quarrying and transporting this stone must have been a major undertaking, especially considering that the city walls were approximately 1.6km long, often 2m or more wide and that the lower courses at least were constructed of massive, metre-long blocks of limestone.

In order to support the wall, wooden stakes were driven into the soggy ground to act as foundations. This must have taken thousands of trees.

It is easier to build a Roman city in places like Cirencester or Bath, where good building stone is easily accessible. It takes real determination to build a stone city in a place like Gloucester.

Another section of the Roman city wall found in King's Square in the 1950s.

The Gates

Like the walls, the four gatehouses of the city were rebuilt in stone by the new citizens of Glevum. So far, two of the gatehouses have been found by archaeologists: the east and the north. The north gate, found in 1974, proved to be an internal square structure made of substantial limestone blocks.

Sadly, in a familiar story for Gloucester at the time, rather than preserve and protect this fascinating part of the city's history, it was destroyed. The photograph shows it being taken apart to make way for yet another cellar.

Today, archaeological remains of such importance would not simply be removed by builders, every effort would be made to leave them in place.

The east gate of the city was found at much the same time as the north and, like the north gate, it was an internal gate constructed of huge limestone blocks. The reconstruction drawing (overleaf) gives some idea of the scale of the structure.

Part of the Roman north gate as excavated in 1974.

Dismantling of the Roman north gate.

Gloucester MP Mrs. Sally Oppenheim (centre) is seen receiving a petition to keep the recently uncovered Eastgate in Gloucester on view to the public. The petition was organised by Mr. and Mrs. Christopher Smith, who are seen here with Mrs. Oppenheim. Story P.12

Like the north gate, the east gate was due to be demolished, in this case for the construction of a new cellar for a Boots store. But, following a public campaign, the remains of part of the city wall and the gate house were preserved. The *Gloucester Citizen* article (opposite) from 1974 reports on the efforts of a Mr and Mrs Smith, who managed to gather some 3,414 signatures on their petition calling for the protection of the remains. Thank heavens they were successful.

The remains of the Roman and medieval gatehouse were saved along with part of the Roman city wall and these can now be seen via a viewing chamber in front of Boots. Sadly, a considerable length of the city walls was still destroyed to make way for what is now the cellar of Boots.

Opposite page:
Clockwise from top left:
The Roman city east gate;
An article in the Gloucester
Citizen, 6 *September 1974*
(permission Reach PLC.);
The excavation of the east gate in
1974. *(Permission Ted Wilson)*

The Roman gatehouse as it is
today in Eastgate Chamber.

The Waterfront

Outside the walls, the city extended westwards as far as the River Severn. The remains of the Roman waterfront have been found in a number of locations.

In 1972, a substantial stone platform was found below ground on Lower Westgate Street on the site of Archdeacon Flats. This is thought to be part of a large stone-built bridge.

The stones visible are probably part of the buttress and wing walls of a bridge very similar to other examples of Roman bridges found in Britain.

The main westward road of the city, the 'Via Principalis', ran from the western city gate downhill between large stone buildings and onto this bridge, which must have been a sizable stone structure and very striking.

The Roman road beyond that ran along a causeway over Alney Island and off beyond Over. We do not actually know how many branches the River Severn had at that time. There may have been one bridge, but there may have been two or even three.

Roman stone platform found at Archdeacon Flats.

Reconstruction of the Roman bridge across the Severn.

Outside the Walls

A suburb extended north-east of the city, along what is now Lower Northgate Street and London Road. The buildings in this suburb were more modest than those within the walls. Those that have been found by archaeologists front onto the road rather like terraced houses. A good example was excavated in 1971.

This building had a veranda fronting onto the street, so may have been a shop or warehouse. The archaeologists also found well-preserved, timber-lined drains. Verandas and good drainage seem to be a feature of Roman Glevum – the Romans were clearly adapting to life in rainy, flood-prone Gloucester!

The most recent evidence for the Roman suburbs was found in 2018 during building work for the new bus station, just off Station Road. Work revealed the remains of a Roman building.

Below: The excavation of the Roman building found in 2018 beneath the new bus station. (permission Cotswold Archaeology)

Reconstruction of the Roman building found on Northgate Street in 1971.

The walls may originally have been entirely of stone, but more likely formed a stone footing for a timber-framed building. The building seems to have been at least 35m long and to have been standing for a period of at least two hundred years, between 1,900 and 1,600 years ago.

The reconstruction drawing shows the building as a timber-framed warehouse or similar. In the background, we can see the walls of the city with a suburb extending out of the north gate. The River Twyver is shown flowing along the southern side of the building.

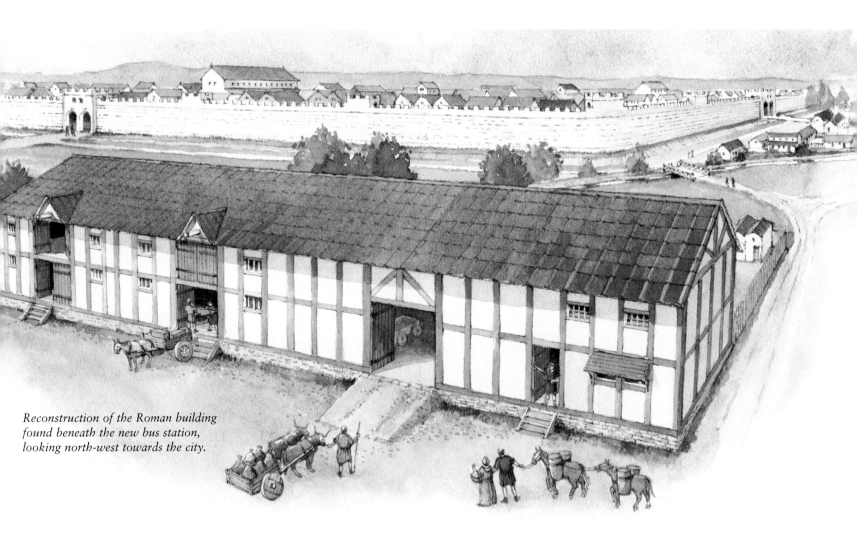

Reconstruction of the Roman building found beneath the new bus station, looking north-west towards the city.

Amphitheatre

One question that has exercised archaeologists for some time is: Where is Gloucester's Roman amphitheatre? You may have seen the amphitheatre in Cirencester, which survives quite well. Gloucester was an important regional centre and so is likely to have had an amphitheatre of its own. Roman amphitheatres were large oval structures, containing tiers of seats set around a central space. That space was used mainly for gladiatorial combats, combat with animals, and public executions. Such events were usually sponsored by wealthy citizens. Whilst amphitheatres in the Mediterranean world were often imposing stone-built structures, those found in Britain tend to be on a much smaller scale and are often constructed mostly out of earth.

Local historian and archaeologist Nigel Spry has suggested that Gloucester's amphitheatre was located south of the city, near to what is now Brunswick Square. This theory is based upon the evidence from historic maps, which show an oval enclosure in this area that historic sources suggest is very old. The enclosure measured about 108m by 60m, which would be consistent with the size of known amphitheatres elsewhere in Britain. The enclosure fits as being the potential amphitheatre for various reasons and most archaeologists agree that Glevum must have had one somewhere, but without excavation we may never know for sure. The reconstruction drawing is based on Nigel's research and shows the amphitheatre with the city in the background. Amphitheatres were usually located away from cities because they tended to attract rowdy and antisocial behaviour, which the civic authorities were keen to keep at arms' length.

Opposite: Hypothetical reconstruction of Gloucester's 'lost' Roman amphitheatre.

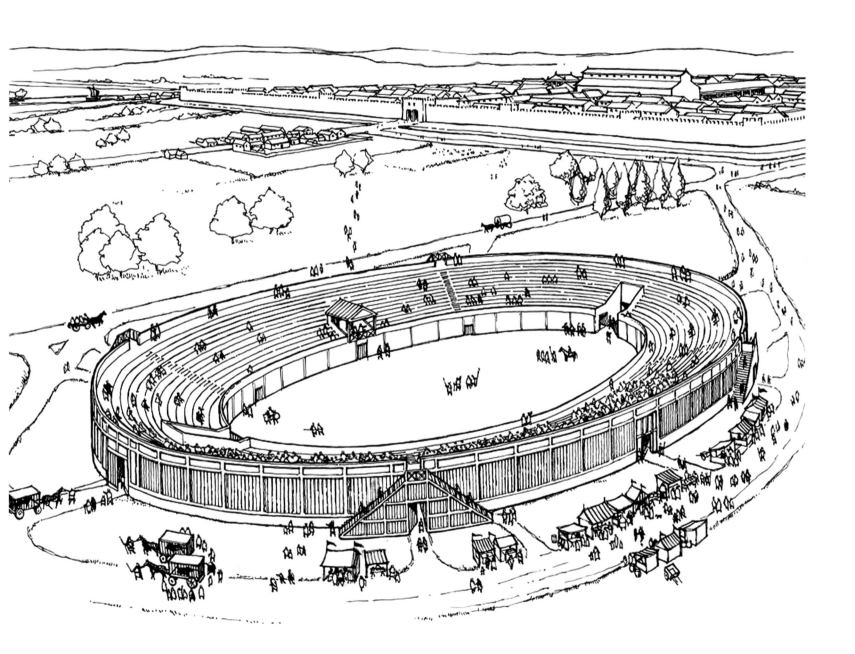

Roman Glevum to Saxon Gloucester

After the Roman period we come to the Dark Ages. Strangely, in all his years drawing reconstructions of Gloucester, Phil has never done any drawings of this period (at least not any he's happy to publish), so our discussion of Saxon Gloucester is going to be fairly brief.

In the late Roman period, the population of Gloucester seems to shrink substantially and it ceases to survive as an urban centre. It may, however, survive as a political and religious centre.

In the seventh to ninth centuries, Gloucester seems to develop as a predominantly waterfront settlement, focused towards the Severn. We know that an earlier version of St Mary de Lode Church and St Peter's Abbey (the modern-day cathedral) were in use during this time. We have also found the remains of Saxon buildings and reused Roman buildings from this period.

An excavation on Commercial Road revealed the remains of a Saxon building– made using recycled Roman masonry. (permission Gloucestershire County Council Archaeology Service)

In the later Saxon period, the late ninth and early tenth centuries, settlement seems to shift back within the old Roman walls of the city. This is almost certainly because of the Danish invasions of the late ninth century AD. Gloucester appears to be re-established as a 'burgh'; a type of fortress, and the city was to become, for a while, the capital of that part of the Anglo-Saxon kingdom of Mercia not conquered by the Danes.

The city was ruled by Aethelflaed, daughter of Alfred the Great. Initially, she ruled jointly with her husband, Aethelred the Ealdorman of Mercia. But after his death, she continued to rule English Mercia, a queen in all but name. She is referred to in Anglo-Saxon texts as the 'Lady of the Mercians'.

Archaeologists have found evidence for resettlement of the walled area of the city in a couple of sites. The first evidence was found in 1968 in Southgate Street (the same excavation that found the Roman forum – see p.32). There, archaeologists uncovered a well-preserved building constructed largely out of wattle.

These remains, which are very similar to structures found in contemporary York and Dublin, probably formed a building fronting onto Southgate Street with some kind of animal pens to the rear. This structure, and another found in Westgate Street, have both been dated to the time of Aethelflaed's rule and are the best archaeological evidence we have for the reestablishment of Gloucester as an urban centre and fort in the late Saxon period.

Well-preserved remains of a Saxon structure found on Southgate Street in 1968. (Permission Henry Hurst)

Invasion

Into the end of the Saxon period, Gloucester remained a place of some importance and was a royal centre. Edward the Confessor used to visit regularly, staying at his palace in Kingsholm.

The Norman invasion of 1066 was to have profound implications for Gloucester, as it did for the whole of England. The man charged with running Gloucester on behalf of William the Conqueror was called Roger de Pistres.[*] As well as sheriff, this gentleman was also the Castellan of Gloucester castle.

'What castle?' I hear you cry. Today, of course, Gloucester does not have a castle, but the city did once have two: the 'Old Castle', which dates from the Norman period, and the 'New Castle' which is a little later but really not new anymore.

[*]Also known as Roger d'Ivry and 'Roger the Sheriff'.

The Old Castle

According to Domesday Book,[*] the Normans, on arriving at Gloucester, pulled down sixteen houses and began construction of the first castle. This was presumably undertaken by order of Roger de Pistres, who was clearly not concerned with being popular. It was probably a simple bank and ditch enclosing a corner of the walled city. This is referred to as a ring-work type castle and would be similar to early castle structures in London, Winchester and Exeter.

Importantly, the Normans were building the castle inside the Saxon burh (the old Roman walls). This obviously means it was easier and quicker to build as two of the walls were already there. But by placing the castle inside the old city walls, they reduced the risk of those walls being used against them. The Normans, of course, were more concerned about rebellion from the local population than external threats.

* Which was essentially a tax survey undertaken in 1086.

Interestingly, Domesday Book suggests that the Old Castle was extended, perhaps around AD 1087 or a bit later. It seems that another eight houses were demolished for this. This extension is likely to have been for the creation of a motte, an artificial hill, with a wooden keep on the top. This would have transformed the castle from a 'ringwork' into a 'motte and bailey' castle and probably annoyed the locals even more.

On the previous page is a drawing of how the motte and bailey castle may have looked. The reconstruction is based on archaeological excavations and observations that took place in Barbican Road, Commercial Road, Ladybellegate Street and within Blackfriars Priory.

The layout of the castle is also based on other examples from elsewhere in the country for the siting of the outer bailey and entranceway. The motte is sadly no longer visible in Gloucester. However, it survived for many years and was actually used by the defenders of the city during the Civil War.

Unusually, the motte was destroyed not by overzealous builders but by archaeologists! It was removed by the Gloucester Roman Research Committee in 1934. The committee, as the name suggests, were concerned with understanding Roman Gloucester and they removed the Norman motte in an attempt to find the city walls. This is just the sort of thing that modern-day archaeologists find exceptionally frustrating!

In 1984, archaeologists excavated part of the castle bailey and found, abandoned in a rubbish pit, one of the most

important artefacts ever discovered in Gloucester: the remains of a 'tabula' gaming set. Tabula was a medieval board game and a precursor to modern backgammon. The entire set had apparently been dumped in a rubbish pit within the castle, probably after it had been broken.

The board originally had a single-piece wooden base made of ash. The upper sides and panels of the board were entirely covered with bone fixed in place by small iron pins, some of which survived.

The Tabula set being excavated in 1984.

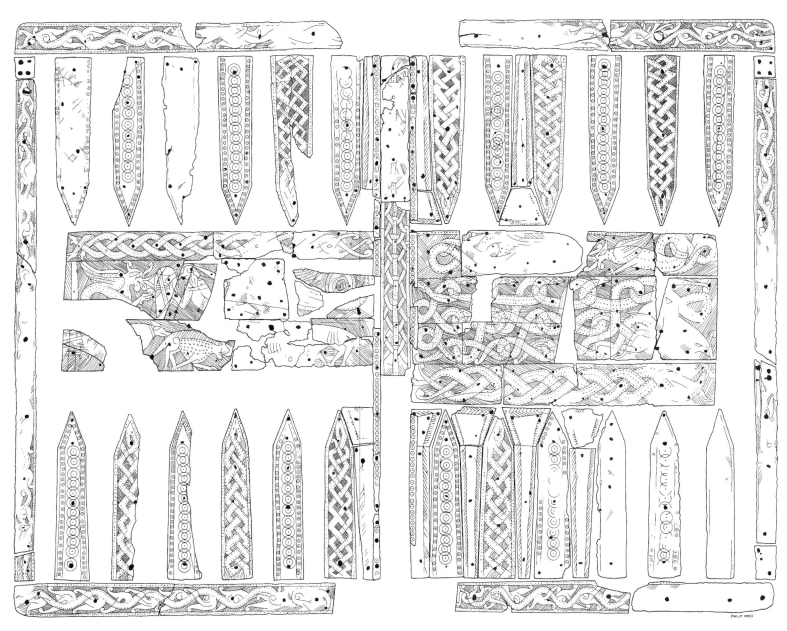

The surviving fragments of the tabula set.

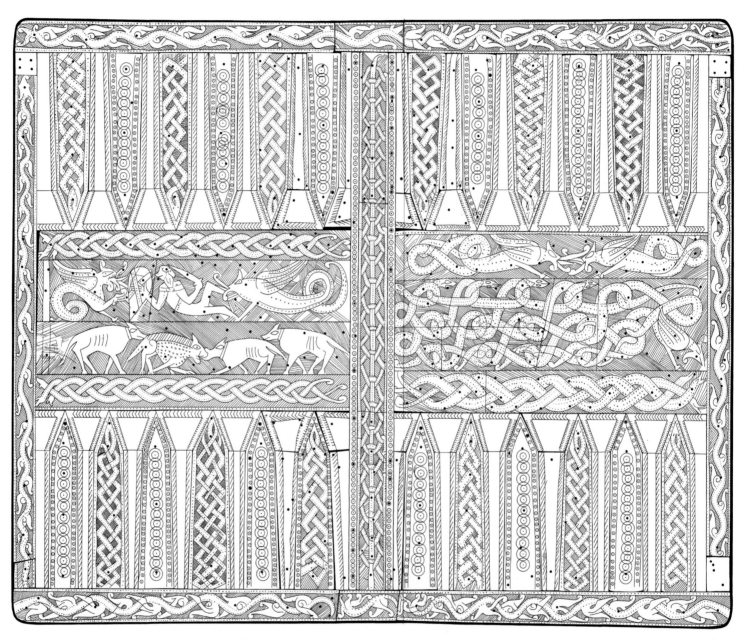

How the tabula set may have looked when complete.

The general layout of the panels follows that of a present-day backgammon board. The thirty counters, or tablesmen, are made of red deer skull or red deer antler (fifteen of each).

All the counters are decorated with carved pictures in relief. Each picture is unique, with a wide variety of themes represented, including astrological signs and biblical events. The counters are carved in a Norman style, while the board reflects an Anglo-Saxon artistic tradition.

Because this is the only complete tabula set ever found, it is of international importance and can be viewed in the Museum of Gloucester – it is well worth a visit.

The old castle probably went out of use by 1120, although its use may have overlapped with the new castle.

One of the counters, showing a centaur with bow.

All thirty of the counters.

The New Castle

Building of the new castle began between 1110 and 1120. This was on a new site nearer to the Severn (the location today of the former prison). It was probably built by Walter (Roger's son) who had now taken over as castellan (as well as being Constable of England – a busy chap!). By 1143, it was owned or managed by the Earls of Hereford but following a failed rebellion in 1155 the Crown took direct control of the castle.

The stone keep was the first structure, built by around 1120. An inner bailey was then constructed, with a main gate tower and bridge being built in the 1180s. By this time, the Old Castle had been dismantled.

The heyday of the New Castle at Gloucester was really during the reign of Henry III (1216–72). Henry had his (rather hurried) coronation in St Peter's in Gloucester during the first Barons' War[*] and retained a fondness for the city for the rest of his life.

While in Gloucester, he stayed in the castle and made a considerable number of improvements.

He constructed:

> chambers and a chapel for the queen (Eleanor of Provence)
> rooms and a hall for his son Edward (the future Edward I)
> a chapel for himself
> a buttery and kitchen
> as well as various other buildings

[*] A civil war between 1215 and 1217 essentially between King John and many English barons about rights, law and Magna Carta. John died in 1216.

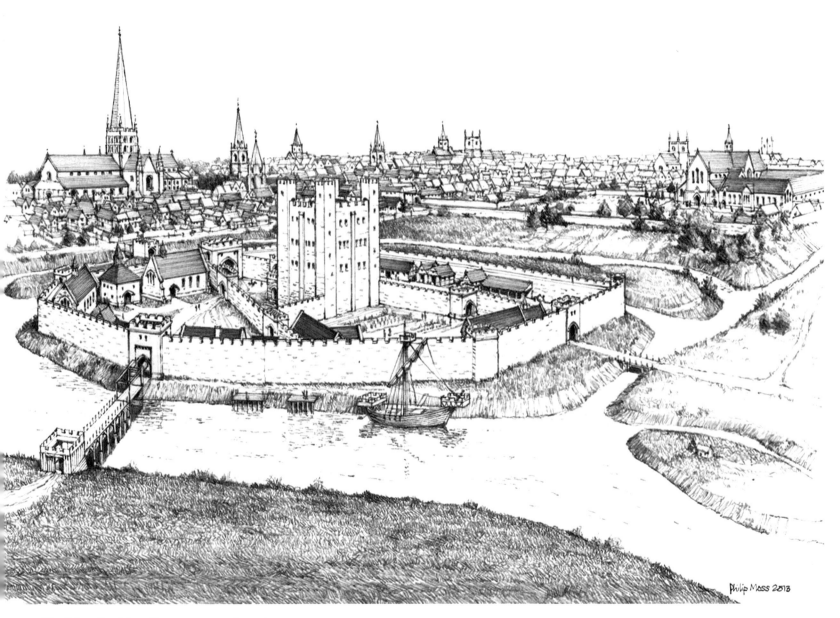

The 'New Castle' at Gloucester, seen from the west.

The castle itself changed hands a number of times during the Second Barons War,[*] as did the city, which attracted the personal attention of Simon De Montfort for the barons and Prince Edward for the king. This gives some indication of how important Gloucester was deemed to be.

After Henry's death, the castle's fortunes waned. Edward I granted the castle to his mother as a kind of dowager payment, as did Edward II to his mother later on. No reigning king was ever to live in the castle again, and in the reign of Richard III (1483–85) it was turned over to its subsidiary role as a prison. Ultimately, the castle was demolished in the late eighteenth century and a new purpose-built prison was constructed on the site.

[*] Essentially a rematch of the First Barons' War in 1264-67 between Henry III and a group of barons led by Simon De Montfort, eventually won by the royalists.

Clockwise from top left: Part of a medieval doorway uncovered by the works in 1985; augering inside the keep. (Cotswold Archaeology); the castle keep under excavation in 2015 (credit Cotswold Archaeology).

The castle disappeared from memory for two hundred years, until in 1985 the Ministry of Justice decided to build a new extension to their prison. Ironically, the Ministry of Justice were something of a law unto themselves and did not need to get any kind of permission before they started building. They duly dug up and, sadly, destroyed large parts of the castle's curtain walls that had survived just below the surface. They also uncovered some tantalising and beautiful remains, like this carved stone doorway (opposite).

These works showed that while the castle did not survive above ground, there were very well preserved remains below the surface.

In 2015, new plans were being considered for the redevelopment of the prison site. This gave an

The western wall under excavation, the archaeologists are stood upon the old wall of the keep – the repair work is visible in front of them. (Cotswold Archaeology)

opportunity to dig a number of trenches across the site. Amazingly, the remains of the castle keep were discovered very quickly. The walls of the keep were massive, at least 3m wide, and they survived just 60cm below ground level (actually beneath the prison basketball court). Based on the results, the keep would have had an external length of about 30m and a width of about 25m. This compares well with some of the most important castles of the time; bigger than Rochester and Canterbury and beaten only narrowly by the White Tower at London. So, this was certainly a significant and important castle when it was built.

Archaeologists also found that the western wall of the keep had been demolished and then rebuilt using huge stone blocks. From historical sources, it seems likely that this was done in 1336 when a survey indicated that the wall was ruinous and in need of repair.

The reconstruction drawing on the following page shows some key elements of the castle: the keep surrounded by various buildings set within the inner bailey. The main castle gate opened to a causeway, which crossed over two defensive ditches to the north-east, following the line of a now lost street called Castle Lane. To the west was a bridge over the Severn onto Castlemeads (which, as the name suggests, belonged to the castle).

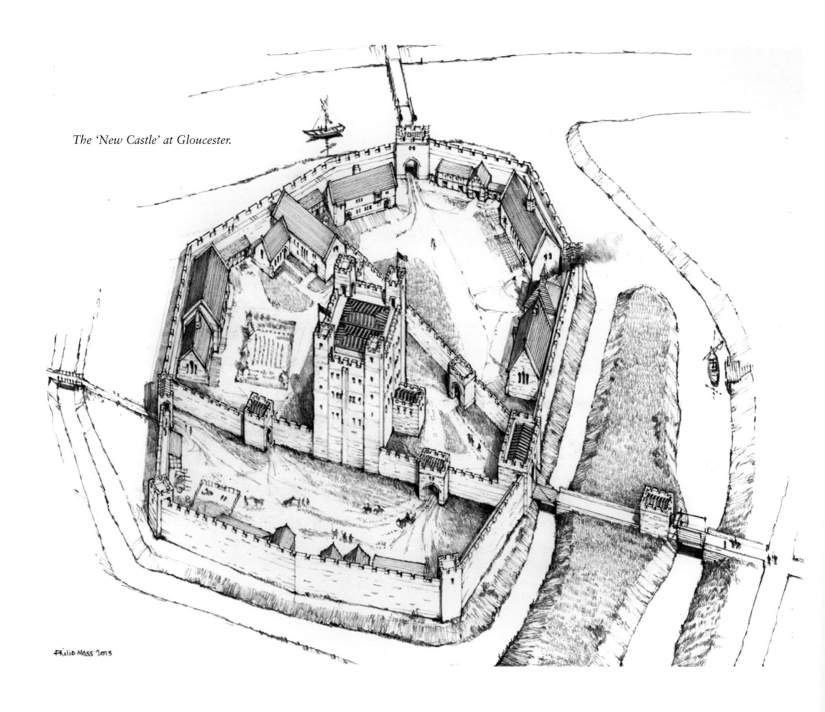

The 'New Castle' at Gloucester.

The East Gate and Kings Walk Bastion

As well as improving the castle, Henry III invested heavily in the city's defences. Given the trouble he had had with the barons, this was understandable.

The excavation of the east gate in the 1970s (already mentioned on p.43) uncovered a projecting D-shaped tower, one of a pair, on either side of the gate. They were attached to the front of the Roman walls, which were presumably also repaired and improved at a similar time.

Excavation of the King's Walk bastion in 1969.

The Eastgate excavation in 1974.

*The east gate of Gloucester
in the thirteenth century.*

The bastion seen from above during excavation.

Henry III also oversaw the addition of several towers around the circuit of the medieval defences. As with the east gate, these were projecting D-shaped towers, which were attached to the Roman wall. One such tower was excavated in 1969 before the construction of the King's Walk Shopping Centre. It is known today as the King's Walk Bastion.

This drawing is looking south along the line of the city defences as they would have looked in the thirteenth century. The bastion is visible in front, the east gate can be seen in the background.

Like the East Gate chamber, the King's Walk Bastion has been preserved below ground, but in this case, there is no viewing window. The bastion chamber is located beneath some shops in the King's Walk. Gloucester locals will know that there is a metal panel within the walkway that lifts up and, down some stairs, you come across the surprisingly sizable remains of both the Roman city walls and the medieval tower.

Tours of both sites are arranged and run by the Museum of Gloucester, with some in partnership with the Civic Trust.

Tours of the Eastgate Chamber and Bastion take place regularly between April and September, while the Bastion also opens as part of the History Festival and Heritage Open Days events programme.

Tickets for all events and tours can be obtained from the Museum of Gloucester website, museumofgloucester.co.uk.

The bastion in the thirteenth century – looking south, towards the east gate.

The Medieval Bridges

At some point in the twelfth or thirteenth century something rather odd happened to the River Severn near Gloucester. A second channel of the Severn broke through Alney Island and became the eastern channel of the Severn, which we are familiar with today. At the same time, the original channel of the Severn began silting up, with its riverfront being pushed north-west and presumably shrinking. By this point the old Roman bridge was probably broken.

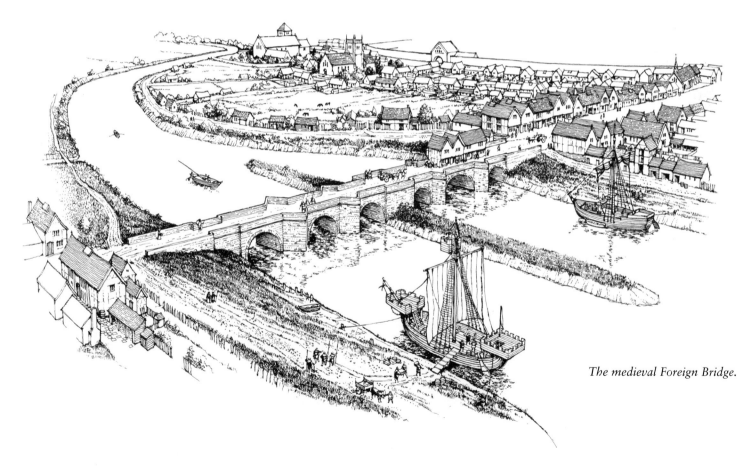

The medieval Foreign Bridge.

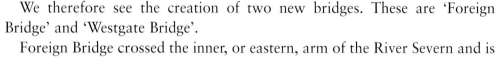

Left: The top of the Foreign Bridge found in 1973.

Below left: The massive arches of the medieval Westgate Bridge found by archaeologists in 1972.

We therefore see the creation of two new bridges. These are 'Foreign Bridge' and 'Westgate Bridge'.

Foreign Bridge crossed the inner, or eastern, arm of the River Severn and is in a similar location, but slightly further west, to the earlier Roman bridge. It was found by archaeologists in the 1970s; a large stone-built arched bridge that still survives beneath the tarmac of modern-day Lower Westgate Street. The reconstruction drawing is based on the results of that archaeological work and historic maps.

The original eastern channel of the Severn was known in medieval times as the 'Little Severn'. Later, it was called simply 'Dockham Ditch', by which point it was almost completely silted up. It was finally filled in the eighteenth century and the ground has gradually risen around the bridge, eventually burying it.

Beyond Westgate Island was Westgate Bridge, which was built in the thirteenth century and has been rebuilt and added to a number of times since.

That bridge was also discovered by archaeologists in 1972. It was exposed within the fabric of later structures during the building of the modern road bridge in that location. Constructed by the middle of the twelfth century, the bridge had five massive stone arches, a gatehouse and a drawbridge. Very sadly, these remains were largely removed.

Medieval Gloucester

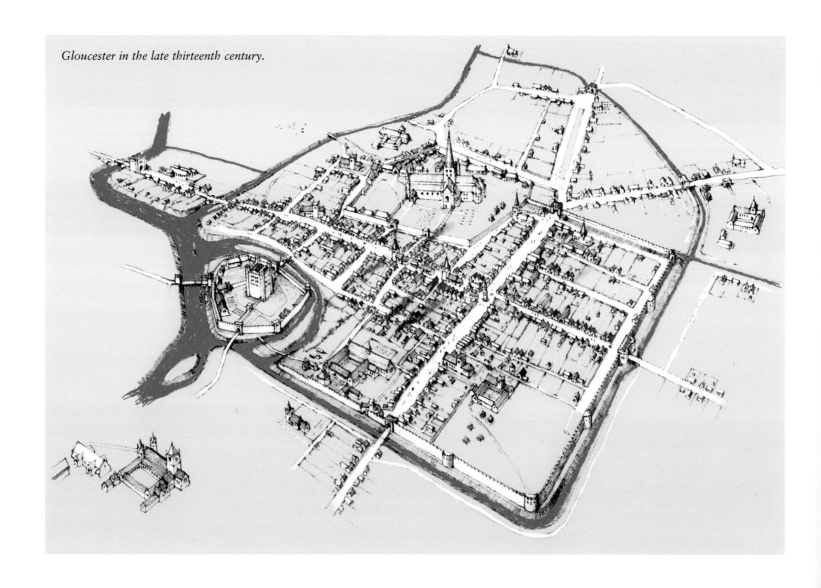

Gloucester in the late thirteenth century.

The drawing opposite shows how Gloucester may have looked in the thirteenth century. The castle is visible in all its royal grandeur. Westgate and Foreign Bridges can be seen either side of Westgate Island. One also gets a vivid idea of how many monasteries and friaries there were in the town: Llanthony Priory in the south, Blackfriars, Greyfriars, Whitefriars, St Oswald's and of course, St Peters. It is also striking how many churches there were in Gloucester at the time, many of which no longer survive: All Saints, St Mary De Grace and Holy Trinity Churches are all now gone from Westgate Street, St Kyneburgh's chapel from the Southgate and St Owen's from just outside the walls. Very true indeed was the saying, 'sure as God's in Gloucester'.

Gloucester Cathedral is one of the best-loved buildings in the city. It's odd then to think that when it was built it was an abbey (or, more correctly, an abbey church). Construction of the abbey church that survives today was begun by Abott Serlo in 1089, and must have replaced an earlier Saxon minster church in a similar location. The reconstruction drawing shows the Benedictine Abbey of St Peters as it would have looked just before the dissolution of the monasteries in 1538. The abbey church was rebuilt and extended on a number of occasions over the course of the medieval period and what survives today is a complex mix of styles, extensions and improvements spanning the twelfth to fifteenth centuries.

The Abbey of St Peters (now the Cathedral) as it may have looked in late medieval times.

The abbey church was enclosed by a large walled area (now the Cathedral Close) which included the great court where much of the day-to-day life of the abbey took place, the inner court (which was located by the abbott's lodgings), a cloister and an infirmary. On the south side of the church (right in the picture on p.71) was the lay cemetery, which served as the main burial ground for the town of Gloucester in the medieval period. The cemetery remained in use until the eighteenth century and is now a rather pleasant picnicking area. The east end of the abbey grounds must have been rather peaceful, containing an orchard and the monks' cemetery. This was a community within a community in the medieval period and it would have quite rare for the normal people of the town to enter the abbey grounds. Following the reformation the abbey became a cathedral and Gloucester was consequently upgraded from a town to a city.

Apart from the cathedral, the Gloucester Blackfriars is one of the best-preserved religious houses in the city. It was founded in 1239 on the site of part of the old castle (see p.55) and Henry III was a major benefactor. The Blackfriars (Dominicans) were a preaching order and they established their house in the middle of Gloucester to be close to the community (this is what marks them as different to monks, who often seek isolation). Like all such houses, the Blackfriars was closed down during the dissolution of the monasteries.[*]

After the dissolution, the priory buildings were at different times variously a mansion, a factory for woollen garments, an independent chapel, the offices of the *Gloucester Journal* newspaper, a malthouse, a mineral water manufactory, a school, a granary, coach house, dispensary and printers. Thankfully, in the late 1950s, the Ministry of Public Buildings and Works undertook the lengthy task of acquiring and restoring the various parts of the fragmented Blackfriars Priory.

[*] Undertaken on the orders of Henry VIII between 1536 and 1541, the dissolution saw the closure of all religious houses in England and Wales. Some of the buildings continued in use as churches or Cathedrals (such as St Peter's in Gloucester) but the majority ended up in private ownership and were demolished or converted to other uses.

Blackfriars today.

Llanthony Priory as drawn in 2000.

The buildings that survive at Blackfriars today include the priory church, the cloister, the scriptorium, library and dormitories. It is a beautiful and exceptionally well-preserved group of buildings and well worth a visit. Today, Gloucester Blackfriars is owned by English Heritage and managed by Gloucester City Council. It is used today as an event space for weddings and the Gloucester Beer Festival, of which I like to think the friars would have approved. Most importantly of all, Blackfriars is a major venue for the Gloucester History Festival!

A site that survives less well is Llanthony Priory, which was located to the south-west of the city, on land now divided by the Gloucester and Sharpness Canal. This was an Augustinian Priory, founded in 1136. It is more properly known as 'Llanthony Secunda Priory' or 'Llanthony by Gloucester'. Its parent house was 'Llanthony Prima', located in the Black Mountains in Wales. The Gloucester house was established when the prior and canons were forced to flee Llanthony during a rebellion in Wales. Llanthony by Gloucester became independent in 1205 and, having prospered greatly, absorbed its mother house in 1481.

Llanthony was, at the time, one of the great monastic landowners in England and Ireland and became so important that the court of Henry VII stayed there twice in the early 1500s. Between them, Llanthony Priory and their rivals, St Peter's (now the cathedral), owned the majority of Gloucester. Why then, as it was so important, is so little of the priory visible today? After the dissolution of the monasteries, the priory became a private house and survived until the English Civil War, when the site was largely demolished; in part because the owner was a Royalist, in part because it provided cover for any attacking force, and in part because it became the focus of an artillery duel (never good!). When the dust had settled, all that remained were a few buildings that had formed two sides of the priory's 'great court', and a tithe barn.

The reconstruction drawing shows the priory as viewed from the west. This was drawn in 2000 and more recent research suggests that the church was probably further north-west, so the drawing is incorrect. That said, it does give some notion of how imposing the priory must have been in medieval and Tudor times.

For many years, the site of the priory has lain largely neglected, its buildings closed and unoccupied. Today, the remains are looked after by the Llanthony Secunda Priory Trust. The Trust has done a wonderful job of protecting the remains and bringing new life to the site. A recent National Lottery-funded project has seen two of the historic buildings restored and brought back into use as lecture rooms for the nearby college and as event spaces. The site really does look wonderful now and has some excellent interpretation – it is well worth a visit.

Llanthony Secunda Priory today.

Normal Life

Of course, most medieval buildings in Gloucester were not castles or churches, but small houses and often rather basic houses at that. While well-to-do merchants and their families lived above their commercial premises in the main streets of the city, other, less fortunate, residents lived in crowded tenements along the many narrow side alleyways. Historic sources tell us that in Gore Lane (modern-day Bull Lane) and Scrud Lane (now Cross Keys Lane) accommodation could be rented in property described as available for use as a cottage or a stable or both! The reconstruction drawing gives an impression of co-habiting with your livestock in the less-desirable Gloucester neighbourhoods.

Interestingly, these properties were actually found by archaeologists in 2016. Historic maps suggest they were still standing as recently as the 1920s.

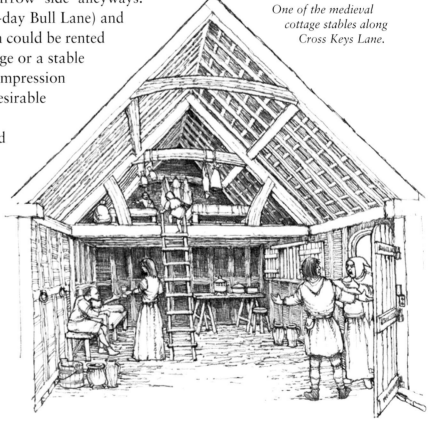

One of the medieval cottage stables along Cross Keys Lane.

Archaeologists excavate the cottage-stables on Cross Keys Lane. (Permission Cotswold Archaeology)

Tanners' Hall

Medieval Gloucester was also the focus for a lot of industries, some of which were rather unpleasant. Perhaps the least pleasant was the tanning industry which smelled – a lot. Unsurprisingly, it was mainly located to the northwest of the city and away from the settled area. In the thirteenth century, Hare Lane was also known as 'Tanners Street'.

In the medieval period it was typical for particular professions to group together in companies or guilds to protect their business interests. The Company of Tanners in Gloucester is probably one of the older such organisations in the town.

The Tanners' Hall.

The reconstruction drawing shows a building called the Tanners' Hall, which was built in the thirteenth century. This building probably had a ground-floor undercroft with a hall at first floor level. The evidence suggests that it was originally privately owned but came into the ownership of the Company of Tanners at some later point. It would have been used by the Company of Tanners for official business; meetings and social events, generally. Interestingly, later on in the seventeenth century, the building was actually used industrially for tanning, so the industry remained in the same part of the city for some centuries.

The remains of the Tanners' Hall have been ruinous and decaying for some years. Recently, however, they have been repaired and incorporated into a new building development. The best result for any historic building really, is that it should be used, so this is a good outcome.

Tanners' Hall today. (Permission: Cape Homes)

Later Use of the City Gates

During the seventeenth and eighteenth centuries, the defensive need for the city gates had largely passed (with the exception of the Civil War). They were by this time the responsibility of the city corporation (essentially the council), which found other uses for these large and solid stone structures.

By 1588, the east gate of the city was being used as a 'bridewell' or 'house of correction'. The north gate was the city gaol. The reconstruction shows the gate in the eighteenth century. A luckless prisoner can be seen in the foreground, while to the rear of the gatehouse, the spire of St John's church can be seen.

Reconstruction of the Northgate as it would have looked in the eighteenth century.

The medieval north gate of the city probably had its origins in a rebuilding of the Roman gatehouse. Unfortunately, there are no contemporary detailed pictures of the gate, but one authority has suggested that it may have resembled the Micklegate in York.

The room above the gate was used as a city prison from at least the sixteenth century, housing convicted felons from among the lower-status inhabitants and visitors to the city. Higher-status burgesses were usually detained in the Booth Hall in Westgate Street. Vagrancy and other petty offences were often punished by public whippings through the streets of Gloucester. The length of the journey depended on the nature of the crime; a minor offender would be whipped to the Wheat Market in Southgate Street and back again. More serious offenders would have to endure their punishment during a two-way trip along the length of Westgate Street from the Cross to Westgate bridge.

By the second half of the eighteenth century, the prison was so overcrowded that the prisoners were allowed to get fresh air and exercise on the roof.

The gate was demolished following an improvement Act of 1781.

Hidden Gems?

26 Westgate Street

Not all the important monuments in Gloucester are associated with kings or emperors – some are simply beautiful and unique buildings constructed by the people of the city.

No. 26 Westgate Street, in the heart of the city, is one of the largest examples of a timber-framed townhouse in England. It is a sixteenth-century merchant house, greatly enlarged and remodelled over the course of the sixteenth and seventeenth centuries.

Like many timber-framed buildings on Westgate Street, its frontage was altered in the eighteenth century so that that it is not immediately clear that this is a timber-framed building at all, although timbers can be seen at the top right of the building when viewed from the street.

The real joy of this building is the timber façade, which is only visible from the narrow alley called Maverdine Lane. Even then, one can only see the structure from below. This reconstruction drawing gives a far better overall impression of the facade. In the fifteenth and sixteenth century, much of Gloucester's city centre would have looked like this.

Clockwise from top left: 26 Westgate Street in the sixteenth century;
26 Westgate Street in the eighteenth century; 26 Westgate Street east elevation.

30 Westgate Street

This is a typical example of the town houses found along the gate streets in the city centre. No. 30 Westgate Street was a seventeenth-century merchant's house. Westgate Street itself was, from medieval times until the Industrial Revolution, the core of commercial and retail activity in the city. Properties fronting onto this street were in high demand because they were guaranteed a large amount of passing foot traffic. This was, until the 1960s, the southernmost point at which you could cross into Wales by foot – so it was always busy.

This building had five storeys including the attic, with a cellar underneath, which had separate access to the street for the delivery of goods. We know from archaeological investigations that an earlier medieval building on this site also had a cellar and this would have been fairly typical: if you walk along Westgate Street today, the majority of the buildings will have cellars beneath them that extend slightly out into the street, so a lot of the ground below the Westgate Street pavements is actually hollow.

30 Westgate Street reconstruction.

33 Westgate Street as it may have looked in the fifteenth century.

33 Westgate Street

Another Westgate Street merchant's house, slightly earlier than No. 30. This building is probably fifteenth century.

The reconstruction shows how it would have looked before being refronted (like many other buildings in the city centre) in the eighteenth century. It is a three-storey building that, again, has a medieval cellar or undercroft. The drawing illustrates well how the gate streets must have been potholed with cellar doors every few metres. Not a place to be walking around on a dark night!

Westgate Street contains some of the most important listed buildings in Gloucester and some that are nationally important. At the time of writing, the city council, with funding from Historic England, has begun the Cathedral Quarter project. This is a three-year project to protect and conserve buildings along Westgate Street, the aim being to make the street more attractive to residents, businesses, tourists and investors. For more information see www.cathedralquartergloucester.uk.

The King's Board

Such was the demand for space in Westgate Street in medieval times that much of the centre of the street was built on. There were two churches in the middle of the street, and various other buildings. The sketch on page 83 gives a vivid impression of how crowded Westgate Street would have been.

One of those buildings was known as the King's Board, which was a very unusual structure, built in the reign of Richard II. Its original function is unclear, but it has been suggested that it may have had an official role such as a place for the collection of tolls or taxes. The building was erected on the site of a royal mint that produced silver pennies from the reign of Alfred the Great until the middle of the reign of King Henry III.

No illustration of it is known apart from the small detail in a map of 1712. Various brief descriptions of the King's Board survive but most were written after it was taken down.

The spandrels (the space between the upper part of the arches) were filled with scenes from the life of Christ, and carvings of heraldic beasts were set above the parapet. The roof was surmounted by a pyramid that had a statue at the base of each corner (possibly the four evangelists).

By the Tudor period it became the established site of the cheese and butter market. In 1694, the pyramid on the roof was removed and replaced with a large tank to store water pumped up from the River Severn near Westgate Bridge.

Sketch view along Westgate Street in Medieval times.

*A reconstruction of how the King's
Board may originally have looked.*

The King's Board was taken down following a street improvement Act of 1750
funded by local wealthy subscribers. The materials from demolished buildings
were retained by the subscribers following the payment of compensation to the
owners of the various properties affected. Parts of the structure were re-erected as a
summerhouse in the ornamental garden at Marybone Park in Bearland for Charles
Hyett, who was one of the subscribers. This small structure was later removed to a
garden in Barton Street and moved again in the mid-nineteenth century to Tibberton
Court. In 1937 it returned to the city and can be seen today in Hillfield Gardens in
London Road.

Modern-day photo of the King's Board in Hillfield Gardens.

The High Cross

At the very top of Westgate Street was the High Cross, which was built by the middle of the thirteenth century. It was rebuilt and embellished on several occasions. By 1750 it was recorded as being a stone structure about 34ft high, containing statues of kings and queens of special significance to Gloucester. In the later medieval period, the lower part had been adapted as a conduit for the water supply brought by pipes from Robinswood Hill.

The reconstruction drawing shows the view looking west towards the High Cross in 1735 and again conveys vividly how crowded the gate streets were before street clearance works were undertaken in 1750.

To the left of the High Cross in this drawing is a building known as the 'Tolsey', which was the seat of government for the Corporation of Gloucester. The reconstruction is based on historic drawings. The original Tolsey was removed and rebuilt in the late eighteenth century, this in turn, was demolished in the late nineteenth century; a great shame because it was a distinctive building and a unique part of the city's history.

The Gloucester High Cross in 1735.

The Siege of Gloucester, 1643

With the end of the medieval period, Gloucester had entered something of a quiet phase. The city saw little change between the end of the Tudor period and the start of the seventeenth century. Gloucester was no longer a centre of Royal power; its economy had declined and it was something of a backwater.

That was until the autumn of 1643, when Gloucester became the stage for great events that changed the course of English history.

The English Civil War had been going on for nearly a year and, thus far, 1643 was going the King's way. This time is known as the 'Royalist Summer', because the Royalist field army in the south-west had won victory after victory. The Royalists, having captured Bristol and defeated the Parliamentary field army at the battle of Roundway Down, needed only to take Gloucester before they could turn and march on London and perhaps win the war.

Charles I arrived at Gloucester on 10 August and demanded the surrender of the city. At 2 p.m., two royal heralds approached the city bearing a proclamation from the King. The garrison commander, Edward Massey,[*] allowed them to enter the city and the proclamation was read in the Tolsey (the town hall):

Edward Massey. (Credit Museum of Gloucester)

* The governor or military commander of Gloucester during the siege was Edward Massey. Massey was only 23 at the time of the siege. He had seen service as an engineer and soldier in Holland and Scotland. Amusingly, he had initially tried to secure a Royalist command but having failed to do so at the rank he wanted, he signed on for Parliament as a lieutenant colonel. Despite his young age, Massey was to prove a most effective and active commander during the siege.

Out of our tender compassion to our city of Gloucester, and that it may not receive prejudice by our army, which we cannot prevent, if we be compelled to assault it; we are graciously pleased to let all the inhabitants of, and all other persons within that city, as well souldiers as others know; that if they shall immediately submit themselves and deliver this city to us, we are contented freely and absolutely to pardon every one of them, without exception; and doe assure them, on the word of a King …

> (*Gloucester and the Civil war: A City under Siege*, Atkin, A. and Laughlin, W., 1992)

The proclamation offered pardon for all if they would surrender the city to the Royalists. Two hours was allowed for the answer.

Four hours later a response was sent:

We the inhabitants, magistrates, officers and souldiers within this garrision of Gloucester, unto his Majestie's gracious message returne this humble answer, – That we doe keep this city according to our oathes and allegiance to and for the use of his Majesty and his royall posterity, and doe accordingly conceive ourselves wholly bound to obey the commands of his Majesty, signified by both Houses of Parliament, and we are resolved by God's helpe to keepe this city accordingly.

> (*Gloucester and the Civil war: A City under Siege*, Atkin, A. and Laughlin, W., 1992)

The council and garrison of Gloucester respond to the King. (Museum of Gloucester)

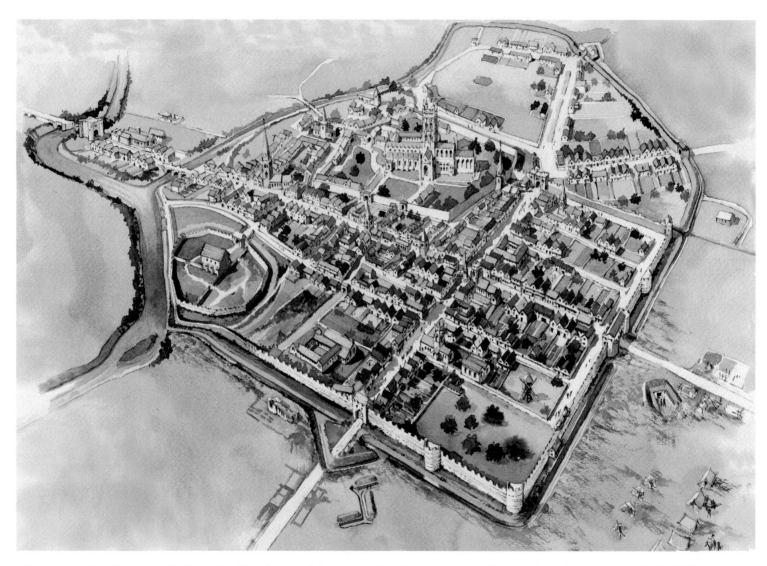

Gloucester during the siege of 1643. A simplified layout of the city produced for a newspaper feature about the city during the Civil War.

Which in short was a refusal to surrender, so the siege began. The drawing shows the defences of the city as they would have looked during the siege.

Until recently, any attempt to map the city's defences during the siege has been rather confused. Thankfully, however, this map was discovered in 2012 in London and has since been purchased by the Gloucestershire Archives. It is hugely important as it shows the defences of Gloucester as built at some point between 1646 and 1653.[*] This is after the siege took place, but the map does show some key elements that are of interest.

Gloucester Castle (then a prison) is shown as being old and ruined. The Barbican Hill (the Old Castle motte) is shown adjacent. External earthwork bastions have been constructed outside the gates and we know that one was in place outside the south gate during the siege. What is striking is that much of the defences on the southern and eastern sides of the city relied on the old Roman and medieval walls. We know that both the east gate and the King's Walk Bastion (see p.65) were standing during the siege and formed part of the front-line defences. The defenders constructed earth banks behind the walls to strengthen them and even filled houses next to the walls with soil to protect against artillery fire.

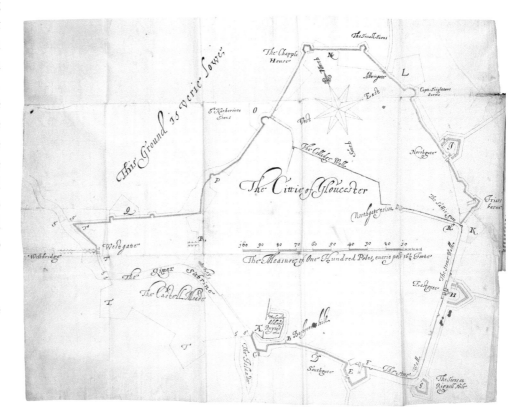

* It also shows a proposed new defensive scheme, which was never built.

*Plan of the Civil War city defences.
(Permission Gloucestershire Archives
Ref D12862)*

The city's Parliamentarian garrison during the siege included two infantry regiments; Stamford's Foot (later Massey's foot) raised in Essex, and Stephen's Foot (also known as the Governor's regiment and the 'Bluecoats') raised in Gloucester. These two drawings show soldiers of both Stamford's Foot and the Gloucester Bluecoats. In total, the defenders probably numbered about 1,500 soldiers.

Soldiers of the Gloucester garrison.

The Royalist forces positioned a lot of their artillery to the south of the city around Llanthony Priory (see p.73) and in a field known as 'Gaudy Green', which is in the general area of modern-day Brunswick Square. These bombarded the city and the defences for many days and nights. The defenders located their cannon on Barbican Hill and the city walls and attempted to knock out the Royalist guns.

The Siege lasted from 10 August until 5 September. During that time, the people and soldiers of Gloucester were able to successfully defend against a Royalist army that may have numbered as many as 30,000. The city was eventually relieved by a Parliamentary field army, led by the Earl of Essex, which had marched from London.

Following the siege, the South Gate collapsed because of damage it had taken. When it was rebuilt in 1644, the following inscription was carved on the arch facing out of the city: *'A city assaulted by man but saved by God'*.

And on the inside *'Ever remember the Fifth of September, 1643, give God the glory'*.

Royalist cannon besieging Gloucester.

Until the restoration of Charles II, Gloucester celebrated the anniversary of the raising of the siege as a public holiday and this admirable tradition has since been re-established, with 5 September being celebrated as 'Gloucester Day'. The City's coat of arms today is based on that granted by the commonwealth in 1653 and shows a lion emerging from a walled crown holding a sword and a trowel, which represent the defence of the city's walls. The motto is 'FIDES INVICTA TRIUMPHAT' – 'Faith triumphs unconquered'.

So, did the siege matter? Well the defence of Gloucester did not win the war for Parliament, but it certainly stopped them losing. By delaying the Royalist forces for as long as they did, the garrison and people of Gloucester removed the best chance for a swift Royalist victory in 1643. The Royalists were never to see a high point like the summer of 1643 again and were to spend the rest of the war increasingly on the back foot. Indeed, one Parliamentary source referred to the people of Gloucester as the 'conservators of the Parliament of England'.

The city's' coat of arms.

The people of Gloucester were fighting for religious freedom, government by consent and the principle that all people, including kings, are subject to law. Their brave defence at Gloucester saved the Parliamentary cause from the very real chance of defeat, and the country from rule by a tyrant. So, with this in mind let us ever remember the 5th of September!

Gloucester, 1750

After the Civil War and the restoration of the monarchy, Gloucester did the sensible thing: kept its head down and commissioned a statue of Charles II. Over the next hundred years the city prospered only modestly. The citizens gradually replaced their burnt-out suburbs and the city walls (already partially demolished on the orders of Charles II) were further quarried for stone. Numerous buildings around the castle were likewise demolished. But the city as it stood in 1750, on the cusp of the Industrial Revolution, would have been fairly recognisable to a visitor from Tudor times.

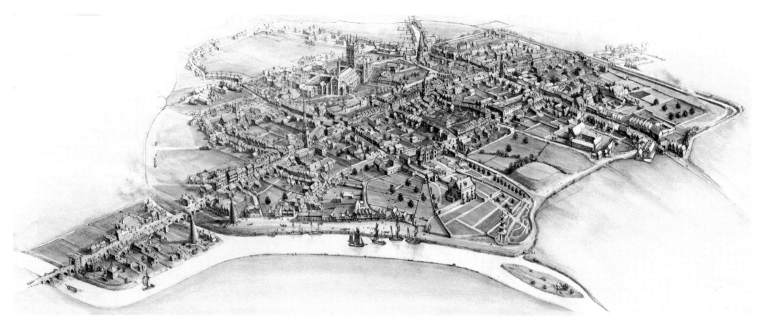

Gloucester as it may have looked in 1750.

The next two hundred years would see a great deal of change: the creation of the docks, the demolition of the Old Castle, the coming of the canals and railway. But, if you know what to look for, the bones of the city have survived and are still visible today. The lines of the first Roman fortress still define Parliament Street and Brunswick Road. The gate streets still largely follow those of the Roman city. The wider street layout – attributed to Aethelflaed – still survives in the heart of the city, and everywhere you look are the churches and chapels raised by Norman and medieval kings. Again, if you know what to look for, you can even see the line of civil war defences around Bastion House, on the corner of Parliament Street. This is a living history; it exists all around us and forms a fundamental part of how we live and what we experience.

Even as this book is being written, new and important discoveries are being made throughout the city. These new discoveries are possible because archaeological remains are now protected as part of the planning process. Whenever possible, such remains are left in situ. If they must be removed, developers are required to ensure that archaeological excavation and recording of those remains is carried out first. These requirements are overseen by the Development Management team at the City Council (also known as the 'planning department'). Any artefacts found during these works are almost always deposited with the Museum of Gloucester, where they become public property and are available for the public to view.

I hope that this book, and especially Phil's artwork, have helped you to better comprehend the story that surrounds you in a place like Gloucester. In understanding, I hope it will help you to value it, to see how precious and vulnerable it is. It is a unique story and a very special one, worth understanding more fully and very much worth protecting.

Creating the Future?

This is a book about the past, trying to understand it, interpret it and explain it. But it's fun and interesting to think about what might have been. Gloucester has, in the last two hundred years, seen several grand building schemes that, had they come to fruition, would have really changed the look and layout of the city today. In the late eighteenth century, early designs for the building of the New County Gaol (later HM Prison Gloucester) proposed that the western perimeter wall be built directly onto the bank of the River Severn. However, it was pointed out that this could provide the prisoners with an easy means of escape using ropes lowered into the gaol from the masts of ships moored against the bank. As a result of this, the perimeter wall was set further to the east away from the river. If the original plan had been pursued what would have been the effect on the road network in the city centre and around the docks today?

Another major event that affected the geography to the north and east of the city was the opening of the Birmingham and Gloucester Railway in November 1840. The company originally planned the route

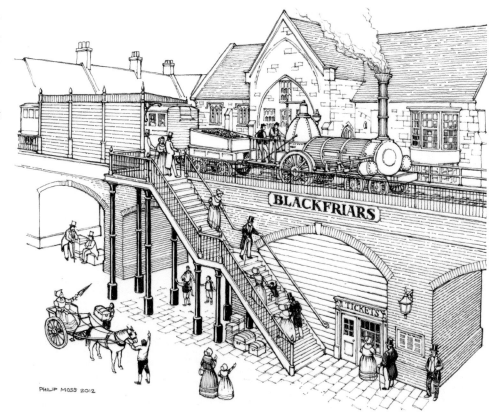

A view of how the proposed station at Blackfriars may have appeared

of the line from the north to cross Barnwood Road to the east of Elmbridge Road then curve to the west on an elevated trackway. The line would then cross Lower Barton Street to the west of India Road and pass over Park Road, Brunswick Road and Southgate Street to a station near Blackfriars Priory. From there it would enter the docks by way of an inclined trackway. It is, perhaps, fortunate that this scheme was not adopted, but also interesting to speculate as to what effect it would have had on the city centre had it been built. Certainly it would have made a huge difference to the look and layout of the city

How the elevated crossing over Southgate Street may have looked had it been built.